Table of Contents

Self Reflection

Apocalypse

Poems for J.

Love Revisited

For Sisters

Poems for Witch Babies

Body Makeup

Layers

Spirituality

Self Reflection

Wants: Part Two

Everybody wants to claim something as their own. People paint their skin with ink to claim the landmass of their own flesh, they raise that flag that says this is mine, and you can only enter if I invite you in. The raging storms inside our hearts are the waters only our vessel can brave—you have to own at least your own heart before you start claiming other possessions . . . I never wanted very much, material things only last for as long as they hold one's interest. I wanted to see the world, travel to little hole-in-the-wall places, I wanted to meet new faces, people who didn't know me, couldn't judge me based on the preconceived notions of their peers. I wanted my words to fly across the pages of everybody's morning newspaper, I wanted to be heard, but no one listens to the voices of youth. The youth of America is wasted. I'm still young but I feel it, the wasting. Something keeps me held back and I'd like to think it's not fear for what's fear but lack of strength? The strong don't fear much. The ones who have the muscle, the money, or the power, or simply have that desperate determination to have more than what they were given, no, those people don't fear much at all. Where did my strength go, my dreams and the innocence of youth; that wild rebellion that makes the elderly shake their canes while we shake up the system? Where did wanting go because I desperately want it to come back. When you have nothing left to want you sit and grow content with what you have . . . I don't know what I want anymore . . . but growing content with the nothing I have is absolutely not an option.

I yearn for independence, freedom . . . to make my mark; leave a stain on the manicured lawns and white picket fences of suburban America, I want to make a mess just because I can and no one can tell me no anymore . . . I want to make my own mistakes because life is so dull without them. I need to walk on the very edge of the ledges you built because life has more meaning when you realize how fleeting it becomes. I want to feel a rush of adrenaline because there comes a point, very soon approaching, when no rush can ever bring me back to life . . . I want to feel something, anything, because there are times very often when I feel nothing . . . and sometimes I welcome the numbness, but not at night when the stars are sparkling like neon flashing; then I want to ignite like fire and burn brighter than those stars someone stuck up in the sky . . .

It should be a crime to grow content and to settle . . . it should be mandatory to grow and change and evolve and accept that its happening is not at all bad. Laughter should be loud, like music blasting from the windows of sky rises. The sun should blare like horns from the taxi cabs in the street, feet should move in rhythm with hearts and no one should ever be alone for very long. This is what I want and wants keep our souls from turning gray. If individuals would find some creativity maybe the gray of the world would go away . . . so let's paint the stark world with vibrant colors again. Let's let the rules that chained us to their misery burn in fiery glowing flames. Let's let the phoenix of our hearts rise from this city's ashes . . . we can claim something again.

Life has no road map. It is as fleeting as your breath when it comes out in tendrils from your nose in winter. It can disappear if you blink too fast. But it is what you make it to be. So don't cower in the back alleys of your fear and let anything or anybody hold you back. Because whatever you want that much is as good as yours . . .

Deformation

She felt just a bit deformed
Like somehow this body of hers
Was too small for the big soul
Trapped inside
        Behind
Ribcage walls and vertebrae;
              Spinal chords
Sinews, tendons, saggy flesh
Draped like a sweater over bone
        To protect that beating, rancid thing
That held a brain of its own.
Her mouth drooped just a little
So her words were always
            Misconstrued
Like the vocal chords inside
          Were severed
Hanging without a plucked vibration
And her tongue hung over her
        Teeth
Lips bitten, bloodied; beauty's
        Beast
Her fingers were gnarled with knobby knuckles
With half bitten nails
Yet held a pencil
        Followed a stencil
But craved to draw outside the lines.
Eyes were planets placed in empty
        Sockets

Caverns to be covered
With diamonds
Glinting,
              Winking
In the corners.
Lids fringed
Hid this monsters truths
While everyone who kissed her
Pulled her petals, tore out her roots
It's no wonder she felt hollow
This deformed little girl
Everyone who knew her dreams
Could only pray
She'd find the key
To unlock her cage.

Trapped

When I was four
I sat on the bench
Beneath my grandmother's fig tree,
And a snowy white owl's feather
Spiraled down from the sky
And fell on my little head.
They say owls are the universal sign for wisdom;
Old wise owls.
I think they're intimidating,
With their wide unblinking eyes
And a head that can spin 'round 360 degrees.
My father says they're silent predators
With massive wingspans
That, when flapping through the sky,
Sound like thunder.
One day hunting,
An owl dove straight at him
And at the last second
Swept itself upwards
So as not to crash into his skull.
Silent and deadly killer,
With talon feet,
Only hunts at night.
Always watching the ground below.
See? Intimidating.
But in the winter,
In that crystalline, powdery frost,
The snowy, white owl waits and listens and is beautiful.
In control.

Was that feather a sign all those years ago?
All those creepy witch people believe in familiars;
Animals that are like a person's soul.
Is the owl mine?
If someone were to look into my soul,
What animal would they see?
What caged beast would await its release?
Would anyone even know how to let her out?

Wandering Girl

I'm a wandering soul
Lost on the side of the road
Got all my feelings inside
'Cause I'm too stubborn to cry

I'll be taking the southbound train
To tomorrow
Trying to regain my yesterdays
'Cause if the past keeps haunting me
I'm certain my future will forsake me

So my soul wanders like a vagabond
Along the dirt streets of rural sorrow
And my heart breaks more with every passing mile marker
Seconds turn to hours in the dust of my lonely morns'

It's discovery for all my time spent in reveries
They take pity on the lonesome traveler
Walking the roads of Americana on her own
Self-examination for failed relations
But I don't need their sympathies

One day all my wrongs will be made right
These days will heal my pain
And some god will surely allot me my mistakes
I'll reconcile with my misery
And before long I'll be on my way . . .

Therefore, what I've become no one could say
What lays ahead remains unknown
Still my empty soul will wander
And it might take a little time
But what I have will only ever be mine
When my soul finds the thing that it needs
Maybe then I'll have something to give
Until the day I decide to return
Don't be waiting for the wandering girl.

The Things I've Built

I took a pencil to an all blank page to create a world I was in control
of
It went from sketchy shadows to bolder lines the stronger I became
I knew what I wanted would not proceed to fall into my lap
So I reached passed those who stood in my way
To take whatever it was that I could grab
I created words that conveyed how I felt
And I didn't care who they'd offend
I spoke from where the seas had swelled
Wrecking havoc on the shores
Of all those countries who denied me entry
I raged like nature at her worst
And nonetheless felt no shame nor guilt
I finished the fortress I had long dreamt to build.

I was powerful in my beauty
And others ran
For I refused to be an object
To be held and contained
I couldn't let them in
For they lied
In hopes of grasping a ghost of a girl
Who ran faster than they could run
Unable to catch up
I left the weak and weary behind.

I chose to turn the leaves over in their mud
So I could become something better
And when I returned you would be in awe

Of the girl you never called
She'd sit higher up on a pedestal
So high you couldn't reach
And my voice would ring out louder and stronger
Than any voice could ever preach
Some days I feel like everything I'd drawn
Should be done over, erased
But then I look at how far I've gotten
And how much I wouldn't give it up
For everything it's taken me
To get passed where I've gone
Nothing you could've given me would make me ever give this up.

For all you thought I lacked
I'd like to have all I gave you back
To safeguard it in my fortress behind my ever sturdy walls
While you sit back and wonder how
All you created crumbled and fell
I'll be ever still creating a world that burns brighter than the sun
And I'll be forever running until there's no place left for me to go.

Whole

It only hurts if I let it
If I suffer silently soon this too will pass
And from my pain the aftermath is always beauty
From my pain come a million and one lighting bugs
Sparkling like stars spread out against the night
I only feel the hunger until I let it subside
My desire stemming from loneliness
My passion whips around like a fire
Out of control
Come appease it just to tease it
Form the clay to fit inside your mold
Until the edges bleed out
Fix the cracks
And peeling plaster
Cover the holes with spackle
It will only kill me if I let it
But it doesn't
So I am stronger
These ghosts can't haunt me if I don't believe
Don't believe in your nightmares
I run but not from monsters
Not from the past
I run not to keep the pace with others
I run but not away
I run only to see how far
I can get before there's nowhere left to go
I breathe to fill my lungs
Not to bring you back to life
So my ribcage walls cannot come down

Unless I let them fall
This body will only break if I let you snap the bones
And since you have taken no more
Than my heart
It's apparent that I can never fall apart.

Fade to Black

Where did all your dreams fade off too?
When you slept through your days who took them away?
Where did all your artistry go?
The colors from your paintbrush ran when the rain fell down
Where did all your passions go?
The fires in your eyes burned out like those shooting stars in the sky
Where did all your memories go?
You wore them like ribbons 'round your fingers
But they untied when he left
Where were they hiding when you went off to your cave
To hide under a rock 'cause you couldn't find the courage to be brave?
They waited long enough for you to show yourself
When you walked into the light the sun burned your eyes
Where did all your loving go?
Mourning doves took off a long time ago
Where did all your answers go?
You never once used to have a question you didn't know the answer to.
Where did the blood that used to pump like ichor through your veins
Dispose itself?
The rivers ran red and you couldn't seem to swim,
They tried so hard to pull you in.
Where did all your childish innocence go?
It was always the most important thing
The rest didn't seem to matter
Now all you used to love only makes you sadder . . .

The Root of the Problem

I felt bones snapping, glass eyes shattering
Lips bleeding, lungs heaving
Dry mouth—cotton
Flesh rotten
Shed my self—disillusioned
To find that beating heart
It's trapped somewhere
There!
Hidden behind ribs
Talons tear
Smoke breath
Incense scent
A droplet of rain could put me out
The flames died out
Amber light
Illuminates the wreckage
On a dirty dock
Ready to sweep what's been left of this body
Out to sea
Mess of carnage
As they hoist sails
No heart
But soul has clarity.

The Sincerest Form of Flattery

Where no one knows your thoughts of pain
The head you hang in shame
Only your eyes held open wide by the pins that pull your curtain
    lashes aside
An imposter in the cloaked sheild of your body
Nobody
Even knows the real you
You don't know yourself
Little child too young to see
Even in your twenties
Shutting down the tongue from sweet
With bitter taste of coffee
Better yet
Bring on the melancholy
And pretend you've never seen a smile
Alone in a crowd of all your friends
Can't grab hold of a hand
To anchor you to this steaming pavement land
Brain just a sponge to soak up that which leaves you stupefied
Milk bones calcified
Bark roots petrified
Your history standing in the hall of a museum
To be put on display and criticized
And a replica of your original art form
Is all you care to be known for
Recognize your copies love
So you are never truly alone.

Winter Face

The heat of a summer could melt the skin right off your face
And come fall you might find a new one underneath the scars
You could run away to a different city
And hope that old seasons fade away
The reflection in an iced over pond
Could resemble a smile
Backed by the winter sun
Or crack until you submerge
Into the dark, hypothermic wet
Fading away, flickering in and out
Like the dying filament in an old bulb
Of a lamp in a dusty Victorian house
The ghost of yourself in its attic
Creaking on splintering rocking chairs
Milky orbs on shadowed stairs.

Exhaled Light

And what caged wonders
Could come out of the box
Of your shadows
If only you opened the lid?

What shells of regret
Are left
Once you've fired off your shots?

What luminous moon
Hangs bloated in what sky,
When you exhale
Why is it that you always sigh?

Speechless

It was easier not to say much,
Especially if you constantly
Felt like you might say the wrong thing.
But chances slip passed
And suddenly
There are very many things you wished
You had the courage to say.
And the days drift away
And with them memories,
You forget faces,
And names,
And what certain feelings felt like.
Months grow to years
And your boat is still safely
Anchored to the dock
Rocking with the wind
But unable to sail the seas.
You just stare longingly at a horizon
As the sun rises day after day
Only to disappear
Once again leaving you cold and dark . . .
Storms rage inside you
And the lighthouse beacon
Lost its guiding light . . .
Grab hold of anything;
Some type of buoy to hold you afloat
In the deep seas of your suffering.
The sun never really sets though,
It just takes its time traveling the globe,

Shedding its warmth on all our skins . . .
Patient ever patient
Is said to be captain of these ships,
So if you'll wait just awhile longer,
Tread this water a little longer,
The sun will come back to warm you . . .

Leaving Home

The urge to leave persists; even when we already know we are in paradise
It's the "grass is greener" syndrome; even if on the other side the skies
    are grey
We could have hanging vines of wisteria and butterflies as big as roses
    in bloom
We could have clear lakes and streams but in this garden we are secluded
And it does our souls not one ounce of good
We cannot be held down
You cannot expect that eternity should be spent in one place
We exist only under the light of a traveler's moon
And if you choose to stay here I will not protest
But I, myself, am leaving even though it might not be best
There are things I need to see
If only for speeding seconds
I can not waste my hours here
Even if your time spent wasting is not wasted at all
You could tell me I'll never find better
But I'll still go looking anyhow
Just because I need to know,
Need to find myself.

Show Yourself

Sift your feet into the sand and make a deep impression
'Cause soon these fields of smashed up stars will be dried up desert
    islands
Leave your mark where others can see it if they can not hear your
    voice
For your face they can not forget if you make them remember your
    name
Desperate people will starve for attention because they are gluttons for
    empty carbs
But those with a healthy hunger strive towards greatness when they fill
    their minds and hearts
Take your paint and fill in the stark white of the hospital walls
Splash the flecks where the mud chokes the reflection of the sun
Douse the flames of their street fires
Ease the pain of self loathing
Forget the insecurities that kept you from letting loose those floods
Take your words to the tops of mountains where they can echo through
    the valleys
And the grasses of savannahs will bend to the roots of oak trees just to
    hear you
Don't deny yourself a place here, atop this mount Olympus
Before you gods and demi-gods are waiting to see your strength
Those who dwell in darkness will rise up to greet you if you show them
    all your light.

Transfiguration

There are a million and one stars bursting in my head
And they bleed their gold dust all over the pavement
There are caterpillars inching their fuzzy little bodies toward some
metamorphosis
And the shedding of their skins mummify me
I am cocooned in the thoughts of others and their reflections become
me
I hang here by the threads of spiders waiting for my transformation
To become the whole of myself
And shed the creation of others
I am a transmutation
And my wings hold the truth
And others like me will find anchorage on petals
And we will pollinate a world
That has simply become a copy of a copy of a mold
I have shattered the mold they held my skeleton in
The broken bits have fused together
I step out of this cast whole and completely intact
For I've spent forever waiting in a cosmos.

La Bohème

La boheme in Montmartre
                    Sipping café noir
Smoking a chain
                    The muse
In paintings of charcoal
                            And oil
Heels ticking
                    Staccato
Like the seconds that pass
In the long afternoons
                    Of leisure.
La boheme in Brooklyn
                    Expressive eyes
Covered by exceptionally
                            Large
Shades
Spread out in Central Park

                    In all her glory
Her world is naked
Untainted
Filled with acrylic light and subdued shade

La boheme
                    With her secrets
Written across her tattooed back

Just about to burst at the seems
                    Of her crimson pout

Her poetry
Aphrodisiac and yet still a poison
                    Her rage
Like lightning in the
                    Summer heat
Her love as ornate as
                    The best wrought iron structures

La boheme in Venice
                    Wearing gilded masks of gold
All there is to recognize her by
                    Her loud and hearty laughter
                                        She
Holds you   captive
For she demands to be heard . . .

Apocalypse

Forgotten City

The air here is stale
It is stuffy; suffocating
I feel a pressure on my chest
A sinking in my gut
To inhale hurts

The buildings in this city are charred
Burned and the ash falls down
Like rain
The streets are empty
Not even the neon lights make a sound

The trash spills out
Flows out from the gutters
Remnants of last year's party
Morning came without the sun

The stars   faded out
Life doesn't wait for anyone

They could've come here once
And breathed in
Filled their lungs
Swelled their brains with vivifying oxygen
But they lay water logged now
Drowning in their murky stagnant streams
A well used to provide the liquid to quench our thirst
It dried up
Like the flower beds that are strangled by weeds

Punctured veins from the thorns
That took hold
Of this forsaken home

Sitting on the stoop, one could have watched the world walk by
But it stopped spinning
In that distant sky
One would have thought it would have been impossible
To even think of a goodbye

This corner of the world stands empty; barren
A desert land
Sheathed in black
Growing colder and colder until it freezes
There are no voices singing
To bring it back to life . . .

Dreamers Weep

There are carcasses of dreams left
From where the sand sucked up the stream
I wish I could see but all there is are empty dreams
Smoke and smog choking the sun
And you stand before your demi gods
With thorns atop your head
Riding your golden chariot until the reins tear the flesh of your palm
Below you all the empty lands:
The deserts parched
The flowers waiting to be soaked
From the rains of the floods.
All our dreams seem to have evaporated
Like the dew on the grass blades in the morning
The pollen thick like burned embers
Coated our lungs and we couldn't breathe
We paraded in their masquerade
Until the streets were littered with star dust
Falling comets that pass only once over a span of too many years
Our dreams are haunted shadows in the alleyways
Nothing more than nightmares . . . .

Throw Caution to the Wind

Wonderland is a madness
A scrumptious dessert to rot ones teeth
Only after they forgot to brush
And tangled in the wires of the streets electric cables
We electrocute to push the addiction deeper through our veins
Harbingers of sweet sensations released into the mainstream
Raucous-causing, hateful sinners
Tossing damnation through the streets
Staring wide—eyed like the passerby
Wide—eyed for it's just too good to feel as though you'll never die.

And I could spend eternity this way
Never watching the sunrise
It sets at dusk anyway
To make room for all the stars
And I don't need the heat of the sun
If the moon moves these waves
All I need is delirium
As the world prepares our requiem.

Eternal Dreamland

Contrite; remembering the dead weather of the Ohio cold
Letters for kindling in the oven of the soul
Burnt brown leaves long forgotten poets would know
Tease the lips of frozen lovers
When they crack like breaking bones knee deep in the snow

Pursed lips won't reveal
The secrets hidden in eyes shrouded with a veil
Death holds a porcelain hand
Macabre melancholy becomes part of the contraband

While the sun beats down in Laurel Canyon
Showering warmth over the poison of the oleanders
A masquerade is vibrantly going on
And glass is smashing in Houdini's mansion
The glittering shards reflect the faces of the new
As they dispose of their hearts
In marble mosaic coffins

Suppressing the beat of pumping blood
For a narcotic medley instead
We could look so lovely
Even if we're halfway dead.

In Dreaming, Slumber

There are no solid colors
Here on this canvas they run together
And the sunshine makes them fade
There are only rotted oak trees in these soils
For the poison's turned these oak trees gray
The concrete is disturbed
By cracks peddlers ran their wheels through
Clumps of tar break free from their asphalt streets and steam
I refuse to sleep for perhaps I'll dream
And then this reality would seem insufficient
And I would want to change what I see in the day
For the neon lights of the dreamed night
The **boldness** of the **vibrancies** that know not the definition
Of F a d e ...
The bursting nectars from lively vines
The marble with its life-line veins
But no cracks to break the face
Carpet grass that cools the soles of feet
And only your back feels the heat of the sun
But when I wake there is none
So slumber bring me rest not dreams
For I'd be sure to hate this place
When morning breaks my window pane
And the midnight storm that rode away on a rogue
Horse
Bit threw the hay of society
No spring breeze
In this humidity
Of awakened reality.

Artisans

The world lacks a certain amount of creativity
We have not seemed to evolve into creatures that can conjure up an
	image
Of beauty
It was said we look at the view and ask why?
But of course when there is no view how many of us ever ask why
	not?
To disparage those who have a sufficient thought
Only makes us look like fools
Since we could not think up the idea sooner
Geniuses can see beauty in a pile of garbage
Free thinkers
Can envision colors where our desensitized society only sets its eyes on
	black
The old format is flat
The edge to life has been sanded down
And we just lust after thrills to override our mundane lives

Life is individual; a blank canvas we stretch
And paint with our experience
Some paint with midnight granite and bone white marble
Others choose watered down rainbows
Chalky, dusty rainbows
Acrylic bold
Others take a needle and paint their layers for keeps so they always
	remember
Some take graphite so they can erase the mistakes like they did not
	happen
We create our canvas to paint a world

But I'm sure of it now
We forgot how to create
Individuality has become obsolete
Destruction seems copious.

Alien

I will never understand the appeal they have
I see no sophistication in their manner
Find their minds senseless caves
And their eyes screwed shut inside sockets

Their tendons; sinewy, attached to meek little skeletons
Skin fleshy, hanging like dusty draperies
Voices formulating foreign words
And no definition for
Peace or joy or love

Their mouths take in bloodied meat by the forkful
Trying to sustain a hunger that will never be satiated
Ever absorbed in their own little worlds
On a planet they will never own

I came here to see what all the fuss was about
Satellite television and radio
Advanced technology
And nuclear bombs
How fascinating their dreams can be

Yet even half asleep they can't dream up
A cure for all the rot they brought.

In Ounces

Misery's inflicting its casualties some more
They're looking for a story to glorify a war

We are always deflecting
Rumors causing storms
A healthy dose of horror
Desensitized is the norm

And it doesn't make a single ounce of sense
That glamour can be found in forms of trash
Seeking rushes of adrenaline
Hollow eyes like store mannequins

Nothing left's corporeal
Covering up the obvious
Gotta blame the innocent
System you second guess

No eyes with a vision
Suburbs of cement
Idolize the gods you let
Form terror threats

And it doesn't make a single ounce of sense
That glamour can be found in forms of trash
Seeking rushes of adrenaline
Hollow eyes like store mannequins

Can you see the sunshine
Through your camera lens
Does it zoom in close enough
To capture smiles of your friends

Can you make Technicolor wonders
Does black and white better fit your mold
Wouldn't it feel better with someone's hand to hold?
The stars seem brighter when they're glittering in gold

And it makes a single once of sense
That beauty can be found behind the trash
Seek a rush of oxygen
To make the hearts come back to life again

Death of Light

Baby the stars are dying
They've been shattered like the filaments in broken bulbs
Split apart like atom molecules
Burst like lungs when oxygen fails
They've been imprisoned behind our barbed wire walls
Chained down only to watch the planets fall

And down on earth I can see them all
Like frayed kite tail ribbons
In tree branches; charred
Burned ash flies out of comet hearts
Meteors crashing like cosmic darts
Hitting their bull's-eye centered mark
Baby the sky is being torn apart

Atlas, hold this Earth closer to the Milky Way
With your strong arms so we can stay
Above the stars caught in the fray
Of solar wars
And lunar tragedies

Under the Tents at Bryant Park

It's running loose out of cages
Wild like doe-eyed dears
Ready to pound the pavement
And overrun the creeks
Madness taking to the streets
War paint painted
Below our bat wing lashes
Lips uttering banshee wails
This is not for the stark white and frail
Running spray can asphyxiation
Over the straight lined brush strokes
Of the mediocre
Creativity and rebellion
Foaming through our clenched teeth
Rabid
Raging
Still engaging
Charming with the words we whisper
Submissive 'till we yell
Howl to the night
They will never forget this sight
Beauty begins to transform
Into something wild
Ragged
And real.

Polite Society

What howls restrained by decorum he said?
What sinister lurkings seek refuge in our heads?
Relinquish the bubbling streams heated by yourself
Intrinsically and only held hostage by doubts

Sought after monsters that smile in the daylight
Hungered after desirable pleasures that whispered their outrage
Soon after you left
What banshees linger in corner alleyways
Dressed for teatime undoubtedly?

I won't keep silent
Shrieking
Ripping
Tearing wounds
And when the moon holds the sea
The light will enter through me
Where I bleed.

Poems for J.

Perfect Autumn Day

We're driving down the parkway with no exact destination, just driving and watching the leaves on the trees blur watercolor spots of red and gold

We skipped a couple exits we probably should have taken, but the road was just one straight path and we didn't feel like turning off just yet

There was this tiny little farm stand where the owner had a funny accent, but we bought pumpkins and marigolds and sunflowers seeds and watched him chew on weeds

We got to an orchard where you could pick your own fill, so we picked at all the apples and the peaches 'till are stomachs would be full

We saw a grassy hill and decided it'd be fun to park the car and roll down the hill until leaves and twigs braided their way into our hair

We kept driving like that for hours just enjoying the day, spontaneously taking turns to see where we would be

Until the sun grew too shy and found its way behind the horizon line, the shadows stuck with moonlight, hung up in the sky

We hit a little streetlight lit cafe and hung there for awhile, holding hands and saying nothing but smiling all the while

When we got home I just couldn't let you leave, so I invited you in and opened up my heart, hoping we could stay this way.

Creatures of Rag and Bone

The moon was this bloated, jaundiced thing
Just hanging haphazardly in a really gory sky
I mean the stars were so transparent
They were merely cellophane skins of diamonds
The smell of the sea was putrid
Some fetid thing rising up and across the ashy sand
The cast of light was so sickly dim
I was happy for the clouds to pass over and make it gray
There was just something about the night that was deathly terrifying
Perhaps it was the fact that I could barely get my voice above a
    whisper
I was just too scared to speak that audibly
And the nape of my neck was clammy
That feeling aroused when you just know someone's watching you
But every time you turn around there's no one there
Well we walked the beach under the gray of night
As bile rose in my lungs
And there were things I could have said but
I was just too preoccupied with getting back to the house alive
It was stupid really because there was no danger
But shadows play games with the mind
And just that something about the evening
The sickness of that moon
Made me feel not so comfortable with holding your hand
And I didn't quite want to let you in
But I was too on edge to be alone
The house was empty and the sea breeze swept the curtains
Made them billow and howl like ghosts
So I let you stay and put on a kettle of tea

And it screamed with steam
Then a beam from that not so distant lighthouse
Suddenly caught the pupil of your eye
And for once it wasn't hollow sunken depths of black
And for once you actually smiled
And I didn't see the jagged edges of your teeth
My bit lip didn't bleed
And my knuckles weren't white
You actually acted like a human being that night
Not some creature of rag and bone
With a skin draped loosely
Over your soul.

La Vie en Rose

Where were you when the clouds dissolved
And broke apart like molecules
To show my eyes the rising sun
To warm my aching bones

My teeth shattered
As they clenched down hard
On pieces of your
Shattered shards

Where were you when the raindrops stopped
Pitter pattering with my heart?

Their petals fell upon my lips
To silence the vowels that would have formed your name
Seems sudden and strange
That the sun would glow
When my cheeks have lost that tint of rose.

Mannequins

Our words were shred like kite tail ribbons
Left to dance on a hurricane breeze
Colorful shards of kaleidoscope glass
Cut out our panting tongues
Our sweat formed sparkling diamonds on our eyelids
Leaving us so we could not see
The blood beneath our cuticles congealed
We ached but we could not bleed.

And the tops of skyscrapers opened up the skies
So steel plated thunder could fill our lungs
Jagged sterns of decaying ships
Floated through the rivers of our veins
Hopeless dreams invaded subconscious reveries
Nothing was what it seemed.

Our cries echoed in some bottomless valley
Our brains, molten lava spewing restless thoughts
Our art, splatters of what used to be our beating hearts
Pleasure replaced by Novocain
Breathing labored without the aid
Of your plastic oxygen masks.

Lifelike resemblance, but just a mold of what was
Our wax like figures without a pulse
But I am still dying until I'm melting
Waiting to fall in love.

Rigor Mortis

It was as if our tongues were severed
In the cavernous holes of our mouths
Our eyes left unblinking
In the abysmal depths of our sockets
Our jaws unhinged where they attached to our skulls . . .

And our milk bones are calcified
Fluorescent in our labyrinth of taut or wrinkled skin
Our joints conjoined with tendons
Attached to the red meat of our muscle

But or senses
Locked in the mortuary of this existence
Can not communicate the beats of these hearts
To our deadened brains

We lay in our morgue
Burying our words
Certain our bodies can no longer feel any love.

Photographs

Camera lenses were your eyes
Flashing like lightning lighting up my skies
Your voice was drum beat thunder
Wild in the canyons
Shaking the earth
Rumbling through me

Tomahawk feathers were your butterfly lashes
Kissing my cheeks like morning dew
Like spring rain
Sparkling on your grass blade hair
As it curled around my fingers

Your feet like roller skates you flew so fast
Dancing through the desert under a sunburst
Or a moon
Floating like seltzer bubbles
And higher still

My heart a dozen swallows
Fluttering their wings
Every time we beat together
And pump the blood in our veins.

Present Tense

Ice wings beat their breath wind through tangled clumps of my hair
Bat lashes with stucco specks fell on cheeks parched of color
Cold fingers, curled like my toes, hide in the pockets of your sweater
But his voice is in my head as I listen to you sing
And another's face is cinemagic as we walk on down the street
And my past and my future are fighting wars with you
And I am pitted between

Let feathers cloud my vision so maybe I won't see
What my hearts constrictions are doing to you or me.

Magic Can't Fix You

Opened wide, mouth like cavern with stalagmite teeth
Fluttering eyelashes, starry Milky Way covering green globe eyes
Secrets like scrawled script on tomb walls, exit from her raw red throat
Poems etched into the small of her back
Stories of ageless importance fill her ears in her nightmares
Feathers in her wood brown hair fall as if from a molting owl
Lithe body bends like weeping willow branches
To touch the soil your tears could water
Your amber eyes could be the sun shining
But you hide behind storm clouds and tornado rushes
Hailstorms bruise your lips
Skeletal branches of pine trees are your sickly arms
You are weak, but not to a gypsy lady's charms
I might try to recite my spells but they could do no better
Someone split your heart in two and you won't allow me to be your glue
So you let the waters lift you up and carry you away
And the grains of sand slough away at your skin
That you burn in the sun
And maybe that would take away the pain
And you would become a different person
Once the old skin peels away
I open my cavernous hole of a mouth
But nothing good enough will ever come out
I try so hard for my globe eyes to show you something better
To hold your secrets in my cave
For my poetry to heal your wounds
I try so hard for my stories to fill you up
To bend to meet you where you lay
Covered in her dirt.

Seasonal

These redwood trees uprooted, like your legs when they acquired the
guts to move
Their branches, as twisted with vines as they were, still struck forth
Like your arms as they reached for someone else
And the soil that kept you planted in the earth
Was rotting with maggots and worms
The rains that watered the veins to your heart
Poured and filled up your lungs
The bark of your skin was peeling away
And the splinters, like razors, pricked my thumbs
The grass below your feet was turning dry like wheat
And the sands of the bank were nothing more than dust
As it filled my nostrils and I could not breathe
The sun scorched the green of your leaves
And they fell like ashes on the autumn breeze
The chill in my bones came in with the cold
Of the winter that killed our sapling growth.

At Dusk

At the violet hour
The bougainvillea wilts
The oleander poisons
The men walk by on stilts
The flowers sweat
Deep between their pollen breasts
Like the women who sweat
Between their legs at night
Entangled in ghost limbs of lovers
Who are never coming back to life

Enchanted stems entwined;
They are vines
Ebbed with thorns these roses are
Martyrdom came quickly
To she who was in love

Disparaging the frost in early spring
The sun in golden armor
Stabs with emerald blades
Sprouts feathers plush upon your mound
Where lying lips silence any sounds

Course wings encase a dying heart
And bite marks trail your neck and arms
They etch across your ivory flesh
Like the ink that wraps 'round his forearms

Marble, raven-black like your eyes
With white veins; bloodshot now
Held open wide
Will never again know the pain of a smile.

A Sudden Downpour of Memories

It's so very quiet and serene
When the dampness from the sea
Starts to shape-shift
Under a pale, pearlescent moon
And the smile of that midsummer sky
Cracks and then it pours

Slicking the gravel
The asphalt
And the tar
Slicking it wet
And it makes you forget
The suffocating heat of the day

The leaves on mulberry trees
Bare only soggy fruit
And these braches want to break
But they only bend towards the wind
The amber glow of streetlamps
Illuminate puddle pools to stomp in

Rumbling engines turn out to be just thunder
And lightning likes to crack sometimes
And tear my heart asunder

But I remember a night when it poured so hard
We couldn't see the streets rolling in front of us
I can't recall how we made it home
As I sit and listen to the sounds of this summer storm

So quiet and serene,
Only rain can wake me from my dreams.

Miserable Me

We're like savages with our damages
Lying to each other, to ourselves
Pull apart our ribcage walls to tear apart our hearts
Sever the tendons, cut off our hands
Never to hold their warmth again
Fixated on some better half
To make us whole again
Souls, heartless behind our layers of flesh
Are always turning away because it's "for the best"
A tonic to wash away the bitter taste
Of sour bile that has replaced
The sweetness of some warm liquor
That slid so easily down our throats
And filled up our lungs

We could fall back into place
Atop the shelf that labels us a disgrace
And we'd take our steps through this misery waltz
Until the music stops

And you'd look a little bit worse for wear
Far more worse than me
I guess it's true
Misery loves company.

The Best Months are Fleeting

There are caterpillars curling in the pollen
An inch thick on peeling white paint window sills
Cocoons just empty shells
Where they lie like the dead in graves
Waiting for some change to come
Awaiting winged perfection
Like angels before pearly gates to Eden
Shedding skins of dead winter
For the morning dews of spring
The warm patter of an April rain
To soak the soils of the coming May
And we sit waiting the arrival
Of marigolds and tulips
The petals of which litter our gardens
As we swing above the emerald grass
Alas
The quick term spring will pass
Into humidity of swelter sun
And we will lounge
Drenched
In cars with windows down
As we roll along the interstate of sound
Searching for the words that will match the rhythms in our heads
Horn blares in the city
And crackle neon; electric
Hum with us in Manhattan
Where the nights are as suffocating as the days
In our journeys for a little bit of cool
Ice cubes down our necks

And kisses hungry for just a touch of ice
We sit out on the stoops of Brooklyn
Watching passerby almost melt on their way by
And our hands held despite the unrelenting heat
And a whistle from the darkened corners of the street
Calling us away for night jams
Where we dance so close we almost fuse
And these are the summer nights
I do not mind giving up springtime for
For in the morning I feel the cool
On the other side of your pillow
And it never occurs to me
That summer could ever end
And fall could be so cruel . . .

Mornings are the Worst Part

The second hand on the clock stopped ticking
Dust particles hung suspended in the air
Sunlight of early dawn muted by your shades
Couldn't reach close enough to even cast a shadow on your face
I looked at you but your eyes were closed
Heard you breathing quietly
But I couldn't say anything that would keep this moment in place
I just watched my moments with you slip away
I got up to leave hoping you'd pull me back
But your arm stayed where it lay underneath the sheets
Drove home with the hum of the heater in my ear
My body tingling where your lips had been
And nothing I do can make the sun go away
I long for our nights that tease and pinch and bite
Now clouds cover where your face once was
Nightmares fill my sleepless nights
But they are the only times I see you
I remember the way you looked at me
At me not passed me
Like I was always the only girl in those rooms
And now your eyes are cold inside
Screwed shut and you'll never see
How sorry I am
And how much I wanted this to be.

Coffee Pot Melancholy

Restless thoughts in my coffee cup
A sickly mud
That sickens all it spills over
Sours like the bitter drug
You poured into the pot.

Heavy and foul on my tongue
Dark grinds melting
And crystalline sugar
Sprinkled from a dirty spoon
Over my chapped lips
Succulent lips
Like fruit rinds
Peeling and bleeding
Left chasing after his lies
As I run to find the milk
To fortify my bones

Midnight nightmares
Swirling down a brown
Oozing brown
Drain
Drained from an IV tube
The lies you poured into my cup
Into me

A diet of liquid caffeine
To shake the dead veins inside of me
Bitter taste of melancholy.

In Conversations

I might vie for your attention
But my attempts seem vain
In this vacuous space
The outcome is plain

I could vindicate your faults
But the effort would create such a strain
The time I spend is useless
The interest is feigned

Your facetious manner's fallible
This drama is a farce
I'm famished for something corporeal
But the provisions are scarce

Your intentions are obscure
I think you just philander
But if you want to prove me wrong
You should quit the pointless banter.

Sticks and Stones Lover

I found the words for the things you couldn't say
But they tasted bitter in my mouth
Not bitter like dark chocolate
But bitter like bile as it comes up the throat
And in those words was a sand bag of hurt
To storm 'round my eyes
And blind
I didn't like those words I found stuck in your teeth
Like dirty bits of food
So I tried my hardest to wash them clean
With rinses of bleach so the colors wouldn't fade
But the black tar of those words just took over like an oil spill
And my wings were weighed down in the mess
Those words formed armies I couldn't keep from attack
As they butchered that thing inside me
I had always thought I lacked.

Mirrors worth Breaking

I wish there were no such thing as tears
So I wouldn't have to watch them leak from the corners of your eyes
And I would never know how they look reflected in mine

I wish the taste of bourbon wouldn't burn
So I'd never have to see you reach for another glass
As you choke back those three little words

I wish that the bass lines were enough
To bring back the beating of a heart
Yet the trill of a ring tone's still enough
To send my membranes scattering a p a r t

It looks like your shadow's enough to scare you away
I wonder if your mirror image is what you thought you would portray

Perhaps if we broke it seven years would fly on by
And my shadows and I would have more worthwhile reasons to
cry . . .

I Beg You to Lie

Take my hands in yours just this once
Kiss the tips and bite the nails
Brush my hair off my face
Go ahead and tug the strands
Grip my neck a little harder this time
Put your mouth to my breasts
Your hands on my waist
Pull me in by the small of my back
And this time don't stop
Press into me till you can't anymore
Breathe with me until you gasp once more
Look me in the eyes
Like I never made a mess
Like we are
Just the way we were
And we'll continue to be
Just lie to me.

Starve a Fever, Feed a Cold

We keep going on like this
And I see no difference
In stopping once we've started
And starting over again

Got our skeletons in closets
Hanging by fish-line nooses
Water's only getting colder
One of us always loses

Hollow hearts
And empty beds
Void of clarity
In heavy heads
Passing up fidelity
While hunger treads so carefully

Nothing more on empty plates
Just shatter the mashed up leftover bits
With the utensils that were always bent
To fit in a mouth where they never fit

Serving up more half hearted schemes
To keep us wrapped up warm in
Half forgotten dreams

Fever chills
And phantom tantrums
To wake me with the sun
But every time I see your face
My sickness isn't done.

Light Footed

I treaded with paper feet
Across your chest
To stomp at the heart
That's been lit aflame
And burn that fire higher
Set it deeper through your veins
My mouth-spout won't put you out
I want to watch this fire burn
Maybe only then I'll learn
How much this fire burns

I let a harvest moon turn red with rage
And I let my beast claws engage
Rip a hole through your face
So maybe then I'd find the face
I recognize

I closed myself behind the garden gate
To listen to its shadows
Their whispers sounded like your breath
When you would exhale after me

I knew I ought to leave but I lost the key
To set me free
So I need to set fire
And watch chaos transpire
To engulf all that has kept me here
Once the ashes clear
Perhaps I'll find my peace
My solid feet.

Departure

The sand in the hourglass seems to finally be running out
Your sweetest words fill my empty heart with only doubt
I know where you are going and it is without me
My heart somewhere deep knows it but my eyes just can not see
I see you in front of me your eyes see only me
In this room I'll deny that you're about to leave
I'll go about my day like my days are all the same
Like no day will ever change
Like maybe perhaps you'll stay
And the clock can tick away all it wants
The minutes fading will convince me this is all my fault
Like I could stop these grains from falling
And keep myself from falling apart.

Everything but . . .

We could have been
If only I had not been
　　So crazy
　　　　So needy
　　　　　　So fill in your
　　　　　　　　Blanks

If only you had told me
Then I would have said
All the things that I held back
Just to keep the peace

We could have been
If only I had been
Anything but casual

I was everything but your girl.

Love Revisited

Love like Arts and Crafts

Paper lanterns illuminate paper hearts
Strung up on telephone wires
Cut like paper dolls
With silly scissors
A faded glow like
Dyed
    D
       O
         W
            N
Embers
Withering away
With their paper Mache
Too easy like tissue paper to blow

                                Away . . . .
Littered hearts in a gutter pool
U n r a v e l i n g veins like ribbons from their spools.

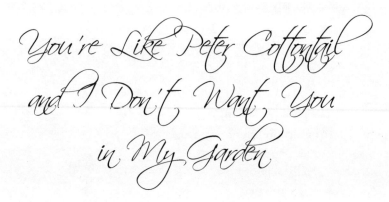

You're Like Peter Cottontail and I Don't Want You in My Garden

If time was thread it's unraveling from the archaic tapestry it came from
If words were roots yours could not take hold in this dry earth before me
If hurt was ivy it's crawling over these crumbling bricks
The wrought iron is rusting, the roses have thorns
Spindly needles from buzzing bees are headed in a fury towards me
If nails are what hold together these walls than this structure will surely
     tumble
And the dry dust that's left after the quake of this storm
Will choke the very lungs we breathe from.

If hate had a face it would almost be pretty in its contortion
If tears were really salt than those seas flood the beach
Where we lay our blanket and basket
If smiles could slice open a face yours is bleeding faster
With every breath you take.

My dreams come in nightmares
My memories fade
A tribunal is forming to decide our fate
There are witnesses to attest to your dark winged laughter
And all the little things you did no longer matter

Some seeds grow to saplings
And others form weeds
And in order for my garden to grow
I need to prune back the debris

Flowers don't bloom without pollination
And I'm sorry if your pollen has become my ruination.

Garden Green

I've been roaming through our garden
Barefoot in the grass
Picking up the petals
From last springs harvest
The purple of the clematis
Matched the violet of your eyes
But I could not get wine to flow
From the grapes off our vines

The hummingbirds that drink through straws
The sugar of the day
Could never know of my distaste
For this garden you so love

I've pruned back all the weeds
I've watered all the seeds
But the berries that grow
In our garden green
Have never been that sweet

Perhaps it's something in the soil
Grabbing hold of all the roots
Or perhaps you've sprayed a poison
But that's something I can't prove

All I know in roaming
Is that all these petals fall
Maybe in this garden
I am not in love at all.

Love Eclipsed

In this ring of endless light
As assemblage of stars collide
Forming a conflagration in the sky
A showering of gold to mesmerize

And in the ivory glow of a marble moon
The smile of a man I knew fades too soon
It withers from the face like spring blooms
At the chill of a transient wind through summer dunes

That searing light creates an exquisite guise
For the likes of darker beings to hide behind
In the corners of this panorama I surmise
Those lunar eclipses could be my love's demise.

From the darkened corners of this earth
I could succumb to endless depths of hurt
But watching the sky erupt in part
Is the sole reason I will not give up

Embers must soon die down and pass
As the world rotates like the turnings of kaleidoscope glass
And life's full of moments that are fleeting; fast
Comets could propel themselves from heights of heaven and crash

They'd land on the beaches where the swell of the seas
Would kiss the scalded bits that lay littering
The sand that was scorched by the morning beasts
And the moon and the midnight would come back to me.

In
    Just
        Spring

E.E Cummings
    And dragonfly wings

Your face is perfect   symmetry
Our hearts beat a fine tuned
        Chemistry

Peel   a p a r t   the dandelion veins
And make a wish when your breath
        Blows the grains

Swerving against white lines
    In tar flooded lanes

A fluttering of wings transpire
When the birds try   to grasp
Pronunciation
    Of
        Your
            Name

Midnight beckons the dawn to ~~break~~
Grass blades await   snowflakes

Bitter cold can not even make
The most slender of branches   snap

And the color of a fire is so profound
As it sparks from the point at which lightning cracked

Above All I'm Forgiving

I write words on a page whenever you crush me
And they flow like the blood inside me
And they swirl intricately blue like my veins
The highways to my heart
And my eyes are wide and chocolate brown
Mirrors to my soul
But mascaraed lashes are a curtain closed
To protect what lies beneath them
It's not my fault I don't trust easily
It's not a crime to wait for love to find me
If you have to ask then the answer's already there
I'm not an open book
To be read and picked apart
So why don't you stay awhile
Get to know me
Discover all the secrets you think you should be told
My dreams are too big to hold
They burst like fireworks
In a too small sky
The electric currents that spark inside
May very well electrocute you if you are not kind
My smile like neon flashing
Can light up your nights
But I'm sorry if I might feel
Like you won't stick around for the daylight
So I'll hold up my armor
Of galvanized gold
And draw my sword of lead

In case I'll need my words
To fight off pain again
But I'll give you nothing but time my friend
So you can maybe erase these scars I have.

August Lover

Augusts' humidity holds leaves in captivity
Stifles the green and the heat turns the leaves brown
They fall like tears of blood from shaking limbs of maple trees
And the sap rolls out the veins through the wrinkled skin; the bark
And the roots come up like creatures in the dark
And howls erupt to make love to a moon
That disappears behind smoke too soon
Fall arrives with a chill
Like the chill that turns these lips to blue
That chills these hands
And their arthritic joints
So they can never hold anything again
And winds pick up to reach your lungs
But snow packs down
To hold your heart
Turns the capillaries to icicles
So oxygen blood can not seep out
Fall comes with out orange and red
A nor' eastern comes to knock your lovers dead
We will long for heated nights
And sweat
Maybe even spring blooms
But we're bound to fall like corpse leaves in autumn
Shoes will crush what's left to dust
And we'll wait for the setting sun at four
Dark and cold and rain to pour
Wash away our smiles
Drown our love in puddles

Promises will get sucked through a sewer drain
And emptied out with disdain
Wait for the mornings when I see my face reflected in patches of ice
Perhaps next summer August will entice.

The Ills of Fall

I didn't pick the apples hanging from some discord tree
Nor carve eyes into pumpkins so for one night they may see
I didn't kiss you in fields of wildflowers where the autumn sun browned
    the leaves
No, I watched our love freeze like the ground
I watched you leave before I could get out any sound
I so carelessly let lost something finally found
And I can't even bring warmth to my cheeks now

Let the apples rot and fall to the floor
And the worms crawl out from the core
Blindness is all I'm asking for
So my lips will never be able to see, the ones they'll never be able to
kiss
I didn't do it
I didn't start this
I don't deserve this
End this.

Octopus

The rats that click inside your head
Are just octopus tentacles
With suckers attached to latch
Onto the matter
That pours from your ears
And foams from your mouth
And runs from your nostrils
Bleeding out
It is your Styrofoam cup
Filled with fluid
Intravenously dripped in a vein
That throbs a little
From a splinters pain
It is the eyelash stuck in a red eye
Poking and prodding
To find its way inside
Don't pull your curtain lids closed please
I want to be that eyelash stuck
To find a way inside your brain
Inside your tunnel corneas
Passed that looking glass
Held tightly in its frame
We could sink low in a submarine,
En route to another underwater plane
This undertow has turned your dry land brain
To sponge
Do you fear a high,
A dive,
A plunge?

Could your T-shirt sails
Travel tear-salt waves
You pour like tea in a Boston harbor?
I think your heart is your best tool for navigation,
But you have barnacles crowding your starboard
These rats that scurry
From the deck
Are your fears from your brain
Running down your neck
Open those eyes and see me
My lips can   heal
Those   wounds
Octopus tentacles
Drove their ink into.

Ariel

I am a fish drowning without her tail
Held captive still by your darkened depths
Who knew they had so much strength to hold?
Boundless lies to mesmerize
Like shiny pearls hidden in clamshells
Yes I am captive, my heart too weak
Bones break; unfortified
How much longer 'till
I sink to the bottom and die?
Still I hold your callused hand
Thinking somehow words
Make us closer friends
Only blue-sea death once glamour fails
Half moons where palms are pierced through by nails
Struggling harder to intake air
Diving deeper into despair
You won't let go with your piranha teeth
You can swim these trenches but
I can not compete
Fingers wrinkling from too much time
Spent in your hellish maritime.

Beastly

I felt my skull beneath my skin, the hollow sockets you can't see in
The razorblades that form a row to bite your lips, the snake tongue
split
A hollow cave with a well-like throat
If you traveled down to find the beating heart
You would drown in the sunken pool

The belly holds a beast
You can hear its howls from the intestine labyrinth
Would you tease it with the scent of your skin
Perhaps entice it with the touch of your hand?
I don't think you'd stand a chance
You'd get swept away in the undercurrent of blood through veins
You'd get lost in the dark, shadowed alleyways of my brain
Your bones would shatter at the first trembling of pain
Your eardrum would bust at the sound of my rain

You keep looking for something that can't be seen
It can't be found in the vessel of a corpse
I feel something tugging at my skin
It scratches and claws but I can't let it in
I think it's a soul that remembers what you're called
But if your name is Love I don't wish to remember you at all
Your music can not break these iron chains

Orpheus, wild beasts ache to tear off your head
Persephone's in Hades so please just let her be
Can't you see true love is dead?

Bookend Memories

If our skins were pages they'd be all discolored
Fragile like diaphanous wings when breezes make them flutter

If the text typed out were the ink colored pools of our pupils
Then tears that burn in the corners would wipe out all our scruples

We'd have nothing better than to pull the strings of lamps and dust our
    cheeks with light
And bring down leather spines from shelves up high and wonder why
    we lied

Heavy tomes weigh down hearts downtrodden
And these untouched memories with gilded edges have means to be
    forgotten

An open window in a mildew room brings only wrecking winds
To scatter torn out pages again

Shoved between bookends we have memories
But we've locked them behind library doors to keep our hearts from
    hemorrhaging.

Zombie Hearts are Always Resurrected

Salt stains the ebony of a heel stuck in the mud
And the rain slips out from underneath the carpet of the clouds
It's only Sunday morning and your thoughts are bouncing rubber balls
Rushing with the thrush of traffic, red lights can't cause their pause
Your eyes are heavy, haggard
And stepping over puddles just doesn't seem to matter
So you press your toe into the reflection of the face you couldn't meet
As you smile towards the strangers passing on the street
Today it's only mandatory to get the paper and the coffee
To sit inside the seedy diner and dream up something finer
Than all the thoughts of yesterday that led you to today
Staring at that face again in mirrored windows and table tops

That man on the corner with his fedora covered mop
Is humming something incoherently
But it sounds like a classic symphony
So for just today it works
To drown out the honking horns and caustic whispers
And everything you scorn

But this afternoon will come the spoon
That ran away from the fork
She decided nursery rhymes were nothing more than jokes
And the evening boa constrictor will come to choke the moon
And she'll let him as she gives off that haunted light,
To illuminate lovers' rooms

And you'll come to his door uninvited
Like a ghost that can't be exorcised
And he'll take off your salt stained boots and put them in the corner . . .

Come Monday morning's funeral you'll again become the mourner.

Farming

Fissures in breaking terra cotta pots
Spill out water like words from your judgmental mouth
There's only hypocrisy in these hydrangea flowers
Petals falling like the wasted hours
No more room for all you doom and gloom
You got the soil drying out the yearning roots
I got my watermelon seeds to last 'till noon
If my dandelion weeds sprout now it wouldn't be too soon

And the stalks of giants could make the sun compliant
With the growth of all the vegetation overgrowing
The rain could drown out the sound of your motor mowing
And I wouldn't give a damn about the grains you're sowing

It's a harvest for the starving but my stomach's full
You should know by now that seasons can be so cruel
Accidental overdose on the pesticides
You have to keep your springtime herbs in line
But my tomatoes taste just fine
Regardless of the intertwining vines

Love
The grass is greener on my side of the fence
Guess it's a show of who has more competence so
Just leave your indignation at the gate
And take your shovel and take your rake!

How'd You Get So Happy with Your Big, Subtle Nothing?

The bile rising in my throat feels like broken shards of metallic words
Possibility for a violent projectile but the object is lodged
Making everything I taste seem bitter
Hard to swallow
A lead weight in an acid stomach that just can not be purged

Esophageal ulcers going off like rockets sending their ashes down my lungs
An entrance where oxygen should breathe honey through my bloodstream
But the fatty cysts have made their home
Cutting off the circulation until I drop blue like lapis lazuli stones

How is it you're so happy, a subtle smile on a pallid exterior
When there is nothing real behind the port holes of your eyes?
Just a subtle hint of something that has long since disappeared
Tell me how it is you're still happy
When I'm hovering over the toilet bowl and my reflection isn't clear?

It was once so easy to let the nausea pass
But volcanic ash
Is bubbling, steaming, rising up
And these tectonic plates won't move enough
To let the lava out

Why'd you stir me up?
Everything was calm albeit stagnant

You've got a cruel, cruel, heart my darling
And I believe I'm choking on it

Olympiad

If it costs that much why spend it
If it was really that fragile why'd you break it
If it felt so good why'd you bruise
If you're the gold medal winner how'd I lose?

If you never tell a lie than speak the truth
Something worth keeping secret between us two
So undoubtedly honest that it's brute
A force to reckon with that you can't refute

If you hold the javelin just shoot
Strike the air so the molecules dilute
I'm jumping hurdles 'til I have shin splints
Falling face first 'til I have split lips

And it's just not enough to keep me happiest
I'll admit I am not the strongest
Swimming laps has left me drowning
These games of silver, bronze, and gold are nothing but confounding

The Demise of a Muse

This is a landscape with a subdued palette
Water colors bleeding from it
Horizon lines are blurred sunsets with a darkness
Stars can not shine from, they only covet

It is a sickness of rueful oils
Rudimentary brushstrokes can't cure
Stretched too taut the jessoed skin
Is a pallor that can't be colored

The touch of bristles is bristling
Graphite lines whistling
As they etch their way with silver tint
To finish their artistic wreck of flesh

The lingering marks of passion last
Even though the frame's been smashed
Decreasing in value substantially
The more you layer the possibilities
For murals with airbrushed oxygen.

Senility Trees

The curvature of your spine
Was like the neck of the lamp you brought closer to the desk
To see the grain better
And even though it was faded
You could just barely make out the faint etchings of a heart with two
    sets of initials
This nightly ritual was habitual
And your eyes were growing tired but you relentlessly set to work at
    trying to see them better
You were vaguely reminded of a memory that perhaps these markings
    were one of your own
But your mind was growing older and you weren't absolutely sure

Your knuckles were the ancient whorls in the wrinkled bark of birch
    trees
And you were transported in your dreaming state to a picnic under
    shady leaves
The wrinkles in your forehead as deep as the indentation in the wood
As you knit together your brow again to gaze harder than you should
It seems substantial to note that certain sights and smells and sounds
Could spark the inkling of a memory and the ink could blot out any
    doubt

What would become of initials in grain when blood ceases its course
    through veins
Is it harder to let go of soils even if they're dry
Would bones uprooted loose their marrow and die
Would joints un-attach from their tendon tethers
Bark skin fall away like molting feathers?

In the Bark of a Redwood Tree

This is the way the world was: with soils filling up our lungs
As the seeds that were planted took root in our arms
And the leaves grew atop our heads where we were freshly bald
And we were watered by those painful tears of slain birds
So once again they could soar
It was freshly mown grass for beds
And dew kisses to keep us warm

The sun lit a fire inside us and we burned up; sap on fire
Coursing rapid like rivers flowing to waterfalls
Plunging into the bright white depths of foam
We were awash in it and we were known
To each other, to the land
The sky, and its stars and moons

I was a part of you and you of me
We were strong limbed redwood trees
The only sturdy branches in a thistle of intertwining vines
Wrapping through the whorls of oaks and testing the strength of time
You and I were timeless
You and I were strong

For Sisters

We were sitting at the corner of miserable, the streetlight flickering on
    and off like a soon to be dying firefly
We sat cross legged; Indian style, meditating on our raucous thoughts
    twisting like television chords
The old black and white kind with alien-tinfoil antennas
The picture in our minds was crackly-fuzzy then turning Technicolor
    rainbow blocks
When you know the programming has been interrupted for a very
    important message
But it was just cars whizzing by with their horns blaring rude and
    demanding to turn down the street first
Like just by honking louder you could get there that much faster
And once you've gotten to said destination what awaits you?
What did you nearly run over to rush over to?
In such a rush to get nowhere, just to another corner of another street
But perhaps the streetlights aren't fading on that side of the block
Perhaps there are some colorful neon lights buzzing like fruit flies over
    dumpsters
Maybe there are musical notes dangling over grocery stores to welcome
    you inside
Jars of things to fit all your pleasures
Perhaps that is a sufficient enough reason to rush

But we were sitting on the corner and we didn't have enough reasons
Enough belief or faith and maybe that's immoral
And maybe the telephone cables have enough electricity
To shock us and we'll recoil
And we'll stop making baseballs out of greasy tinfoil
But for right now we have pigeon feathers

Twirling between middle and forefinger
To tickle our noses
And we'll sneeze out faerie glitter
It's harder for us
Just us two
The kindergarten paste that holds our bones together
Is not as strong as Elmer's glue
If it were simple, something easy
We would not have grown so tough, so callused on our hearts
They would have been soft, squishy, blue-veined things
Not at all so hard to suffocate

I look at you, half of a mother's genes
And worry if you'd feel more comfortable in someone else's blue jeans
I could sit on this corner alone
But could never feel right if it was you
So while you are parked, sitting Indian style at the corner of miserable
Or maybe it's depressed? My eyes are tired from crying for you and the
    street sign's just a little blurry tonight-
I'll sit the same way talking to you listening to your dreams as they
    shoot off into the sky
Like disco-bright fireworks
And maybe we could be the ones to start setting them off
So the colors are a brightness we can control
Instead of waiting for someone else to light up our skies
We could be something better
We could be those stars hanging like charm bracelets in the night.

Won 4th honorable mention in the writers-editors online contest

Birdlike

Feathers sprung from the pinholes where your lashes grew
Rose vines entwined where your veins were blue
Scallop shells were your fingernails
Tucking strands of seaweed hair
Behind a snail shell ear.
Your eyes wide and brown; my doe-eyed dear
Spinning like saucers when the tea pours out
Flower petals fly passed teeth like pearls every time you shout

My own feathers caked with oil slick mascara; thick
And every time I blinked it blocked out the sun, burning like a wick
It seeped into the wells where the oil then pooled
Drowning in veins that swelled storm grey-blue
My fingernails were torn from the quick and bit
And raked through hair burnt like autumn leaves in a tantrum fit
My eyes were slits and hidden beneath
Heavy lids and a mouth that could not get attached lungs to breathe

You were electric perfection on a bed of moss
Atop the sticks and twigs my smile got lost
In our bird nest above the sea-foam green
I somehow felt you were better than me
Someone whose feathers were not a mottled brown
Whose silence somehow transcended sound.

Blood Sisters

The ink you used to spell the words
You couldn't form on your tongue
Are bleeding out from where they're tattooed
On the blanket of your flesh
It's like an inkblot from a fountain pen
Gushing where it stabbed the page
And it's filling the expanse of your back
Like oil seeping through the rivers,
Off the coastlines;
The vein canals to your stormy ocean heart
That keeps twisting like a maelstrom
Sucking the sails from these ships
Whose cannonballs blow you apart

The fleets are forming in the harbors
Can you see the gilded masts?
They're throwing ropes to reel you in
To save you from the blast of waves
That crash to drown you in their wake

We see your words are fading fast
From where they're sketched so deep
Blood promises that mixed with ink
Of black and red and green
I see the scars they covered up
I remember the voice
That you forgot
And I'll sail out to sea
If it means that you'll float back with me

I'll raise one flag
On a desert land to let you know you're safe
And we'll bring color to those promises again
The ones we inked across our hearts
Those shriveled up beating things
That time burned black
With tobacco smoke.

Frankenstein's Hospital Bed

The landscape of your brain's alive
Electric with the cable wires
That stretch across the roads of your open soul
To transmit signals to your heart

But your landmass flesh
Is sinking
In the salt water tears of your ocean
My bouy can't keep you afloat
There's an anchor trapped inside your throat
To keep your tongue from speaking

But I know that brain of yours is thinking
It's sparking with the transformer
And any day it's sure to blow
So before this body heads for black out
Won't you take my shock absorbing hand?
If you fear your light bulb when it starts to flicker
I've got my generator to save your battery again

The lightnings coming quicker
I'm not certain if you'll burn out
But still you launch your kites to the sky
To see if they'll disappear among the clouds.

Live for Discoveries

Someday you'll find, love
That life's what you make it
And you can drive these roads because they're here for you to take
It's so easy to leave behind what causes you pain

The world's like an ocean
With treacherous waves
But I urge you to hoist up those sails
You can beat the sunrise
And the moon and stars will guide you home
And if you find it too dark I will be your beacon light

So many things
You ought to see
So won't you come on and join me please?
Our travels can take us
To the clearest of streams
You can have the reality of all of your dreams
If only you would just move your feet

I'll ease your worries
'Cause I've had them all before
And I've learned
Anything you want is worth fighting for.

Poems for Witch Babies

Witch Baby

Never before have I seen her get so low
Hanging like the blackbirds from the scarecrow
Upside down so the blood rush comes
Faster to the brain cells coming undone
But it's just this way she's happiest
Using cornfields as her catalyst
Sprinkling seeds of dissension
In her crop circle of woe
Overturning cracked clay with her shovel and her hoe
Juxtaposed to corn stalks
She has her canvas teepee tent
And all the gnomes who think they know
She only circumvents
Furthermore her arguments
Will leave you in such disarray
Almost as if a tornado came
To sweep your current thoughts away
In the evening when the thunder comes
I can hear her cawing
And the rustling leaves shake at the sound
And with the rain start falling.

Mother Earth

Did you see what her brain did to the trees?
>They grew like cells symbiotic and the pollen dusted our
>cheeks

The cactus had a flower the color of the iris of her eye
>The needles turned to softer bristles, what fell dead became
>new life

Did you see what she did with the sky?
>Exhaled all her oxygen to make clouds multiply

I heard a rumor that if you sought her heart,
>To catch a glimpse of the beating red would pull the blue of
>your veins apart

I once saw her in the evening trees hanging upside down
>Her toes curling like cashews, her stockings on the ground

She was chanting nursery rhymes in tune with the wind chimes
I knew someone who knew her well
>But never spoke a word

And then one day she just disappeared
>Off to where no one had heard.

Demeter

Silence.
Like cotton wadded up and stuck in the corners of the sky
You couldn't hear the stars twinkle, twinkle
Snow.
Powdered the cheeks of her face
And I walked across her dimples
Her eyes were closed,
She only opens them for the dawn
Sunlight.
Streams through the slots of the iron gate
And waits
For the concrete to appear.

Be a dear? Start the pot of coffee
We'll sit nestled here
On the couch
We overstuffed with our expectations

Gray
Her eyes are still closed
Barefoot across her lips I can feel the tremble
The sigh behind them
Waiting to be released

In due time
        In due time
All will be released

It's just a matter of time
Then our hearts will be appeased

We'll come to rest on a reclining chaise
Hear chirpings
          And twittering
Catch acorns
Before they come to lie
On the spring green shadow
          That covers her lids

Spring will begin

The Pierces

They are druids in white
How did they get the clouds
To allocate the cotton
With which they weave
Billowing fabrics
To snake around their ankles?

They have foliage
Braided through their gold spun strands-
Which enchanted forest have they come from?

They glow like they stole the sunbursts,
And the sunflowers' pollen
A blush to dust their cheeks

I've caught them
        Dancing in the moonlight naked
Running like does over hills
        And howling like wolf mothers
                        Atop canyons

They must bathe in the Milky Way
Make their beds in dew grass

They drink a tonic from a wishing well
And light fires at night to cast their spells

They bang a tambourine and sing along with wind chimes

Fill their lungs with feather wind
Watch them pound the ground with their moccasins

Turquoise rings and rabbit fur
Shed their winter skins in rivers

Make their offerings for spring
Sacrificial lambs to abate hunger
Once again

Witchy druids in white, eagles taking flight

Catch the feather that falls
And pierce your wrist with the needle

            Make a wish
And affix the feather where you need to

Listen for them closely
When the wind starts to kick up the dirt
And the rains start to flood the earth
You'll hear their echoing laughter first.

Body Makeup

Free of Form

If we were only plasma how much freer would we be?
To soar through atmosphere like comets
Coming back around every couple years
We would never know our constraints of skins
And tendons
And ribcage walls
We would never miss the feel of bodies warm
And kisses that bite
And our hearts
We would never be confined behind
The barbed wires of our brains
We would only move and blend together and we would be free of
form

Anatomy 101

Explain to me the inner workings
Of the respiratory system
Show me how the most noxious of CO2
Of human exhalation
Can sink into soil
And travel up roots
And photosynthesize
With sunlight
In leaves
And a breeze
Can carry oxygen to our lungs

And the lungs contract
And again expand
And blood cells
Turn over
As they venture along the vein lines
To a heart

And explain to me
How this heart
Without two lungs
Can not beat

Why two, why not just one?
What happens to my heart
If my ribcage parents
Were to lose one of their twins?

Would the percussion cease with the loss?

Explain to me how one can breathe another in
And the heart beats a little faster
Explain to me how lungs constrict
When blood stops rushing to my cheeks

I'm not quite understanding
Only just mastering this anatomy

Help me grasp the meaning
Of these systems that make up my body

A. Nervosa

Insipid tongues try to coax the teeth to bite
But the eyes are ubiquitous
And the stomach contrite
The lips that pucker at the sight
Berry stains are just the blight
Of the hand

Do understand
I really do try
To get these bicentennial wheels of mine
To turn
The inner mechanics of the frontal lobe
Albeit with grief
Seem to like to work alone

Perhaps I'll just take that there tea instead
And the aorta will halt its rush of red

However, I'm more likely just to go to bed

Vegetable Garden

The compulsory smile given
Tears deplore the stricken
Eyes half closed can not discern
Heaven's azure heights

Lungs can not grasp fully
      Breath
When it's only fanciful at best
      A fallacy

When the next step is only death

Death of suns
Clouds have overcast

Heart walks in a trance
Feet take their stance

Like roots
The veins dig in
Unrelenting in their need to begin

Their journey

To a brain half dead
      Unknowing

Whose skull it is encased in

Layers

Construction on the Internal Tracks

Displaced emotions in the portals of just dredged sewer tunnels
They swell with the rising currents of water flooding the paths
We swim them daily regardless of the fear we may drown
The emotions build
The water grows deeper
The tunnels are dark labyrinthine depths
But we burrow deeper into our system of intertwining tracks

At last
We enter into the light
The pounding against our chests relieved
Sucking in the air last breathed
In by mockingbirds
Mimicking our laughs
-those little lost sounds haunting us in the night . . .

Respite in the middle of the daily grind
Furrow the brow over the Times
Meander once again in the tunnels of the mind
And once again displaced emotions enter
They bite and howl at you
Convinced you'll succumb once again . . .

Electric exertions of subway trains steer you clear of the fray
Gaining momentum in the flooding portals
There's a conflagration forming at the end of that tunnel
You strain against the heat
The smoke swelling
The flood and fire meet

And there's finally a place for those displaced emotions
When you come face to face

Persephone Searching

I entered through the labyrinth searching for the center part
The stalagmites glowed fluorescent in the deepening dark
There were claw marks on the walls juxtaposed to crude art

My fingers caressed the etchings like somehow these walls could speak
The secrets of the ones before me buried in the moss beneath my feet
Voices choked by death in travel—a life's journey incomplete

I pressed forward deeper still into the belly of the beast
Looking for a heart to pound a familiar drummer's beat
But all I heard were the tunnels' echoed howls and shrieks

I heard the bubbling of springs boiling in the dim
Lapping the sides of crumbly walls and exposing skeletons
A man in chains was half alive with sunken hollowed skin

He told me a fool was I to enter here
His gnarled finger pointed in judgment, and his body shook with fear
Beware the one with deep-set eyes, they're only the windows to a vacant
    soul—even though they're blue and clear

I trekked onward not the least afraid of a man who bound himself
I was free of his chains and only searching for myself
To see what beating song was inside a beast who had chose to hide from
    everyone else

And it is when you are focused on a dark path and not looking to your
　　right
That the one you think you needed enters your peripheral sight
With deep-set blue crystal eyes to lead you to a promise of light

And he glows brighter than stalagmites growing fluorescent from the
　　limestone
And he says there is no longer any beast here, if you stay here you'll get
　　lost alone
Wandering aimlessly with no way out of this forsaken one time home

Penetrating eyes keep you entranced and you will follow blindly
Not noticing the darkened tunnels are moving downward and
　　winding
Spiraling faster and you were oh so close to finding
Something akin to a bloody pumping thing with just a hint of Midas'
　　gold
You thought a beast would hide something of that caliber under all
　　that fur
Unbeknownst to you, the most angelic of creatures to guide you
　　home,
Take the best parts of you they warned you a beast would claw at to
　　hold

Should've known the song you were searching for was inside you all
　　along

About Face

1. You failed where your efforts were strongest
You bailed when your solidarity was wanted
Left struggling over some sort of conquest
You need to have over yourself.

Juggling their feelings of conviviality
That seem so hypocritical
When the puzzles are all the more trivial
Your quick response is pivotal.

No one can assure an outcome
That wouldn't leave you undone
You swim out further than you should've
Waiting for that moment when someone will come
Save you.

2. The moments that left you breathless
Are choking you now
As you're pushing towards the surface
For something more than the numbness you feel.

The threshold is bearing down
Where the foundation is weak
Cracked cement tumbling faster
Like a spine that's weak.

And the veins in the ground, upturning
In soils where nutrients are spoiling
Rotting the leaves
Before they are ever warmed by the sun.

3. One by one and two by two
I'll keep pushing right on through
Against your armored crowd amassed
To lunge at me until the nausea passed

Violent projectile of inner demons
Succubus of a heart's desires
Army of shadows in the dark
About face. For a new start.

Spirituality

The River

People think of time as standing still
These people spend too much time thinking
Life is fluid motion; time is a river that is constantly moving upstream
And people tend to try and float there moving with the current
Content people happy with where they're headed are simply ignorant
    to where they're Going
Others fight the tides and swim against the current
Moving backwards whence they've come
Perhaps they liked it better there
Longing for the past
It only makes you helpless
I'm content to swim in the stream where the currents don't affect me
Time does not affect me
It is nonexistent time
Life is overflowing
And when I am done in this stream I will simply head to another
For my arms and legs are limber and strong
I can make the swim to oceans wide and vast
With no regard for time
Not to think of tomorrow or yesterdays
Not even to think of futures, just the now
The overflowing cup of now
The stream that kisses the shore line moves out and then comes back
    again
The deltas of silt that gets re-deposited wherever the tides take it
I will be the silt moving to each and every stream
Until I have swam every sea there is to swim
I have no goal of reaching a horizon
Just for reaching what's put before me

If it takes hold and drowns me I will simply drown
But bob again to meet the surface of another wave to carry me
Whether it be to coastline or shoreline or yet another river
I will still refuse to merely fight the river or grow content with wherever
    it will take me
I will become fluid
I will become the river
Try your hardest to fight against me
Or swim with me
But like any river I can change my course over rocks
I can change my depths
I can be shallow
I can be cold or warm
I can take the silt from the delta
And deposit it elsewhere
But I will be forever moving through mountains and valleys and I will
    be clear.

Out of Nature's Quiet Nights

The night is quiet despite all the worlds' madness
We roll across the open road like bummed out beatnik travelers
The only constant is this open road
So come camerado give me your hand
And travel the open road with me.

Our arms out-stretched to meet the tar
Hot and steamy under the un air-conditioned car
Tires sputtering, raggedly breathing in
The exhaust exhalation of this midnight hitchhikin'

The blades of grass quiver like the arrow shot from the bow
Sent out long and far to coasts East to West then back again
We soak up the sea salt as it permeates our skin
Come my friend let us be lovers again

Drunk on the breath of life itself as it's injected into our veins like
    Benzedrine
High on the rolling hills and dipping low into valleys to find the only
    road there is
Intertwined in the madness of all the worlds' restless souls
Getting lost en route to Mexico

No regard for the amount of miles traveled
Here we're lookin' for no exits
Only entrances
Looking for those massive steelworks
That bridge the gap from our forsaken hearts
And merge our souls wholly

The gravel roads, the dirt roads
The newly pavemented
The white lines blurring
Like the sun as it fades into the night
Let's take to those roads not yet discovered
Keep driving until the sun and moon cease to emanate such light

Such light that keeps us after some common goal
Indignant and rebellious we take to the road
Never ceaseless in our amazement
Of the beauty created indifferently
Without might of man
Out of sheer will
Nature's bountiful harvest.

Bodhisattva

They sat under a bhodi tree
Contemplating the mystery of god
Every god
In all the religions of the world
And they couldn't translate the meaning of nirvana
Perhaps it was something not meant for them to obtain
In an after life
But to strive to achieve in this life
Maybe to sacrifice was in vain
To emaciate to feel pure
One would simply feel hungry
Perhaps the point of starvation
Is to fill the soul and not the stomach
To give up wants is to free oneself from greed
And material things
When one has nothing to need
Isn't he then the wealthiest?
To preach commandments seems fruitless
Who is to command one's heart?
To give freely is better than not giving at all
But to give of yourself is best
To watch and listen is polite
But to stand and fight is courageous
But what is worth fighting for
If the fight is merely to go to war?
When the cause is to prove the other wrong
Is it really worth fighting at all?
And to fight in the name of your god
Seems almost sacrilegious

When two religions fight in the name of their lord
And they only believe in one god
Aren't the two sides then fighting the same fight?
They thumbed through bibles
But found only words
When if religion is spiritual
How can one put spirit into words?
They went to temples and mosques
Built beautifully and inlaid with gold
But outside the threshold
Lay poverty
Collections for the coffer
To buy your way into heaven
Repentance for ones sins
But isn't it a sin to take
But keep from the poor?
All this contemplated under the arms of the bhodi tree
And the bumblebee landed on the petals of the flower
To begin its pollination
And they decided that religion was not all in vain
If one could find that peace is achieved
Through nature's determination
Of producing something whole
Out of broken things.

Zephyr

We are fog and we dissolve like ephemera
Leaf—like growing and falling, tumbling down
Being swept out to sea in the early dawn

We are insufferable creatures creating war
Ripping up the roots
That took hold before we were born

Bhikku traveler men wander the streets of L.A
Searching for jacaranda canyons with laurel leaves
Bodhisattvas looking for their souls' release
Into the rust colored deserts of the plains

Shaman man, head up in the clouds
Pulling the thunder down
From mount Olympus

We are greedy, famished
Insatiable hunger giving way to madness
Corneas dilating wide in bloodshot, bulging eyes

High up on a mountain somewhere in the Big Sur country
One fast move or I'm gone . . .